FLOODS

THE WORST IN HISTORY

BY JENNA VALE

T0204911

Gareth Stevens
PUBLISHING

Please visit our website, www.garethstevens.com. For a free color catalog of all our high-quality books, call toll free 1-800-542-2595 or fax 1-877-542-2596.

Library of Congress Cataloging-in-Publication Data

Names: Vale, Jenna, author.
Title: Floods : the worst in history / Jenna Vale.
Description: New York : Gareth Stevens Publishing, [2025] | Series: World's worst disasters | Includes bibliographical references and index.
Identifiers: LCCN 2024001874 | ISBN 9781482466676 (library binding) | ISBN 9781482466669 (paperback) | ISBN 9781482466683 (ebook)
Subjects: LCSH: Floods–History–Juvenile literature. | Natural disasters–Prevention–Juvenile literature.
Classification: LCC GB1399 .V35 2025 | DDC 363.34/9309–dc23/eng/20240214
LC record available at https://lccn.loc.gov/2024001874

First Edition

Published in 2025 by
Gareth Stevens Publishing
2544 Clinton St
Buffalo, NY 14224

Portions of this work were originally authored by Janey Levy and published as *World's Worst Floods*. All new material in this edition is authored by Jenna Vale.

Designer: Claire Zimmermann
Editor: Megan Kellerman

Photo credits: Cover, p. 1 (main photo) Olha Tytska/Shutterstock.com; series art (newsprint background) Here/Shutterstock.com; series art (fact box background) levan828/Shutterstock.com; series art (cover & caption box paper texture) Suti Stock Photo/Shutterstock.com; series art (hazard symbol) Maksym Drozd/Shutterstock.com;
p. 5 Chronicle/Alamy Stock Photo; p. 7 courtesy of U.S. National Archives and Records Administration; p. 8 BONNIE WATTON/Shutterstock.com; p. 11 (upper) SSKH-Pictures/Shutterstock.com; p. 11 (lower) Jaz_Online/Shutterstock.com; p. 13 (upper & lower) Everett Collection/Shutterstock.com; p. 15 AlexelA/Shutterstock.com; p. 17 VectorMine/Shutterstock.com; p. 19 Wutthichai/Shutterstock.com; p. 21 The Army personnel rescue stranded pilgrims at a relief camp, at flood-hit Hemkunt, in Chamoli district, Uttarakhand.jpg/Wikimedia Commons; p. 23 (upper) Glaucia de Almeida Campos/Shutterstock.com; p. 23 (lower) Nelson Antoine/Shutterstock.com; p. 25 Chinedu Chime/Shutterstock.com; p. 27 speedshutter Photography/Shutterstock.com; p. 29 Zaltrona/Shutterstock.com.

CPSIA compliance information: Batch #CS25GS: For further information contact Gareth Stevens at 1-800-542-2595.

Find us on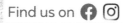

CONTENTS

WORDS IN THE GLOSSARY APPEAR IN **BOLD** THE FIRST TIME THEY ARE USED IN THE TEXT.

WATER OVERFLOWING

A flood is the event of water rising and flowing over areas that are normally dry. Rivers can flood their banks. Tsunamis, or huge ocean waves, can cause flooding in coastal areas. Even rain can cause a flood if there's too much of it.

Some floods are small and don't cause much **damage**. Others are so large and cover so much land that they're considered natural **disasters**. Flooding is one of the most common natural disasters in the world. Large floods can destroy cars, homes, and even entire towns. Floods can hurt or kill people too. There have been many terrible floods throughout history.

⚠ THE YANGTZE RIVER FLOODED IN THE SUMMER OF 1931, BUT THE FLOODWATERS REMAINED FOR SOME TIME. THE PEOPLE SEEN HERE ARE GOING TO THE MARKET IN SEPTEMBER 1931.

THE YANGTZE RIVER

CHINA'S YANGTZE RIVER HAS FLOODED MANY TIMES. SINCE 1870, IT HAS FLOODED VERY BADLY EVERY FEW DECADES. THE FLOOD IN 1931 COVERED MORE THAN 30,000 SQUARE MILES (77,700 SQ KM). THE FLOODWATERS KILLED AROUND 145,000 PEOPLE, AND 40 MILLION PEOPLE LOST THEIR HOMES. THE FLOOD'S AFTERMATH ALSO CAUSED DISEASE AND **FAMINE**, KILLING AS MANY AS 3.7 MILLION PEOPLE ALTOGETHER.

5

WHERE FLOODWATERS RISE

Wherever there's a body of water, there's also a chance for a flood. Rivers, lakes, and oceans can all flood land. River floods are common. In fact, most rivers overflow their banks around once every two years.

Floods happen around the world, from the United States, to Europe, to Asia. However, some places have serious floods more often than others. China's history of flooding is the worst. In the American Midwest, the Mississippi River, Missouri River, and some smaller rivers flood often. In the Great Flood of 1993, both the Mississippi River and the Missouri River flooded, gushing water over nearly 400,000 square miles (1 million sq km).

THE GREAT FLOOD OF 1993 COVERED MUCH OF THE CITY OF DES MOINES, IOWA, SEEN HERE.

MIDWEST UNDERWATER

NINE MIDWESTERN STATES FACED SEVERE DAMAGE FROM THE GREAT FLOOD OF 1993. THOUSANDS OF PEOPLE WERE FORCED FROM THEIR HOMES, AND AROUND 50 PEOPLE DIED. ALONG THE MISSISSIPPI AND MISSOURI RIVERS, HUNDREDS OF **LEVEES** FAILED, ADDING MORE WATER TO THE FLOOD. THE DAMAGE ADDED UP TO ABOUT $15 BILLION. IN SOME AREAS, THE FLOOD CAUSED PROBLEMS FOR AROUND SIX MONTHS.

HOW FLOODS HAPPEN

From too much rain to a dam breaking, many events can cause flooding. The sudden melting of snow and ice can produce river and lake floods. Flash floods, or floods that happen very quickly, can happen when heavy rain causes a lot of water to gather in a narrow space.

Lake floods happen when strong winds push water onto land. An earthquake can cause a lake flood by moving the water from side to side. Earthquakes that happen on the ocean floor can produce tsunamis, flooding coasts with **debris** and causing damage. Even wind from hurricanes can cause a type of ocean flood called **storm surge**.

FLASH FLOOD

CAUSING A FLOOD

heavy rain, persistent storms, snowmelt, **ice jams**	→ RIVER FLOOD
high tides, winds blowing toward shore, heavy rainfall	→ COASTAL FLOOD
hurricanes, strong winds, low pressure in the atmosphere	→ STORM SURGE
rainfall over several days, dam or levee failure, hurricanes	→ INLAND FLOOD
heavy rain in a period of hours, dam or levee failure, debris flows, ice jams	→ FLASH FLOOD

 THESE ARE SOME OF THE CAUSES OF FLOODING. DIFFERENT FACTORS CAUSE DIFFERENT KINDS OF FLOODS.

FLASH FLOODS

FLASH FLOODS ARE ALARMING BECAUSE THEY HAPPEN MUCH MORE QUICKLY THAN OTHER FLOODS. A FLASH FLOOD CAN HAPPEN WITHIN MINUTES OF A DAM BREAKING, OR WITHIN A FEW HOURS OF VERY HEAVY RAIN. FLASH FLOODS ARE ESPECIALLY DANGEROUS BECAUSE THEY LEAVE PEOPLE VERY LITTLE TIME TO GET TO SAFETY.

FLOOD DAMAGE

Floods are dangerous to people, animals, land, and any place people live. Floodwaters can easily drown people and animals. They damage and destroy buildings, roads, bridges, and crops. They can also pollute the water supply.

It may take days for floodwaters to **recede**. Then, buildings and belongings are left covered with mud or destroyed. Water and food could be unsafe to drink and eat. There may not be power for lights, heat, or cooking. Flood damage like this is hard to fix. People may need supplies, shelter, or other kinds of help while their homes or towns are rebuilt.

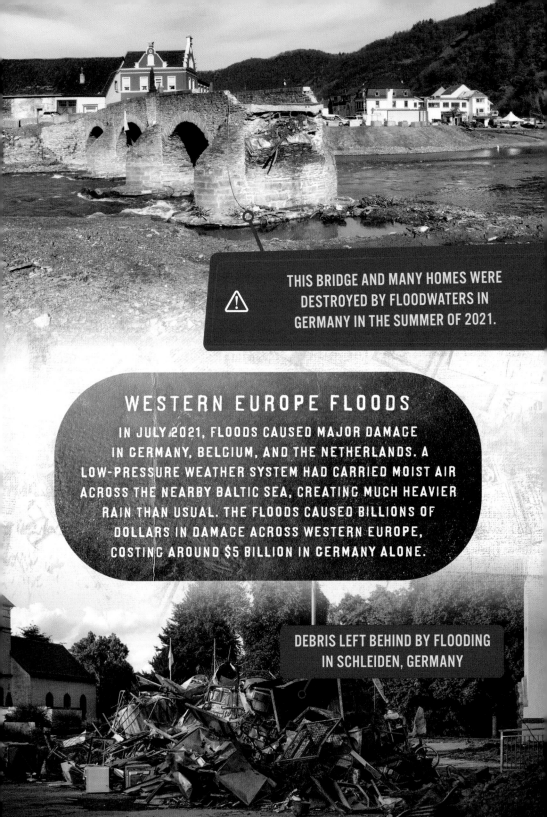

THIS BRIDGE AND MANY HOMES WERE
DESTROYED BY FLOODWATERS IN
GERMANY IN THE SUMMER OF 2021.

WESTERN EUROPE FLOODS

IN JULY 2021, FLOODS CAUSED MAJOR DAMAGE
IN GERMANY, BELGIUM, AND THE NETHERLANDS. A
LOW-PRESSURE WEATHER SYSTEM HAD CARRIED MOIST AIR
ACROSS THE NEARBY BALTIC SEA, CREATING MUCH HEAVIER
RAIN THAN USUAL. THE FLOODS CAUSED BILLIONS OF
DOLLARS IN DAMAGE ACROSS WESTERN EUROPE,
COSTING AROUND $5 BILLION IN GERMANY ALONE.

DEBRIS LEFT BEHIND BY FLOODING
IN SCHLEIDEN, GERMANY

JOHNSTOWN DESTROYED

The deadliest flood in U.S. history happened in western Pennsylvania in May 1889. Heavy rain filled lakes and rivers. A huge storm on May 30 brought even more rain. The South Fork Dam could not hold back all the water, and it broke open on May 31. Twenty million tons (18 million mt) of water spilled out of the dam.

A wall of water up to 100 feet (30 m) tall raced down the valley. It destroyed the town of Johnstown and several other villages. The damage totaled about $17 million, and more than 2,200 people died. News of the flood spread, and the newly founded American Red Cross traveled to Pennsylvania to help.

THE JOHNSTOWN FLOOD'S RUSHING WATERS PUSHED TONS OF DEBRIS DOWN THE VALLEY TOWARD THE TOWN. AROUND 100,000 TONS (90,700 MT) OF DEBRIS GOT STUCK AT THE TOWN'S STONE BRIDGE, SEEN HERE.

DISASTER RELIEF

THE AMERICAN RED CROSS IS A DISASTER RELIEF ORGANIZATION THAT WAS FOUNDED IN 1881. THE NURSE CLARA BARTON STARTED IT AFTER HER TIME LEADING BATTLEFIELD RELIEF EFFORTS DURING THE U.S. CIVIL WAR (1861–1865). AFTER THE WAR, BARTON BELIEVED THE ORGANIZATION COULD HELP PEOPLE WHO WENT THROUGH DISASTERS. THE JOHNSTOWN FLOOD OF 1889 WAS THE ORGANIZATION'S FIRST NOTABLE DISASTER RELIEF EFFORT.

RUINS OF HOUSES AFTER THE JOHNSTOWN FLOOD

CHINA'S YELLOW RIVER

Many horrible floods have happened in China. In 1931, China's Yellow River overflowed its banks. Water covered about 34,000 square miles (88,060 sq km). About 80 million people became homeless, and around 1 million people drowned. The flood also caused famine and disease, killing up to 3 million more people. The 1931 flood was one of the deadliest natural disasters in history.

Before 1931, the worst Yellow River flood happened in 1887. That year, a **dike** failed and sent floodwaters over the land. The water covered between 10,000 and 50,000 square miles (25,900 and 129,500 sq km). Hundreds of villages and towns flooded, and between 900,000 and 2 million people died.

WHY THE FLOODS?

THE YELLOW RIVER GOT ITS NAME FROM THE FINE YELLOW **SEDIMENT** ALONG THE RIVERBED. THE SEDIMENT MAKES THE WATER LOOK YELLOW. IT ALSO MAKES THE RIVER MORE PRONE TO FLOODING. THE FLAT LAND ALONG THE RIVER MAKES FLOODING MORE LIKELY TOO. THESE TRAITS OF THE YELLOW RIVER MAKE FLOODS MORE FREQUENT AND MORE DANGEROUS.

THE YELLOW RIVER, SEEN HERE, IS SOMETIMES CALLED "CHINA'S SORROW" BECAUSE IT HAS KILLED MANY PEOPLE. IT'S ALSO SOMETIMES CALLED "MOTHER RIVER" BECAUSE THE RIVER'S VALLEY IS WHERE ANCIENT CHINESE CIVILIZATION BEGAN.

FLASH FLOOD IN VENEZUELA

In December 1999, flash floods struck the state of Vargas in the South American country of Venezuela. Heavy rain fell over the mountains. The water flooded downhill, causing thousands of landslides. The floods carried heavy sediment and other debris, which made them very damaging. They were so powerful, they changed the slopes of some hills and destroyed 60 miles (97 km) of coastline.

Around 190,000 people had to leave the area, and between 10,000 and 30,000 people died. Hundreds of buildings and other structures were destroyed. The damage added up to around $1.9 billion. It was the worst natural disaster to hit Venezuela in modern history.

FANS AND FLOWS

THE AREA AT THE BOTTOM OF THE MOUNTAINS IN VENEZUELA HAS SOME FAN-SHAPED LANDFORMS CALLED ALLUVIAL FANS. THESE FANS ARE MADE OF ERODED SEDIMENT THAT HAS COLLECTED AT THE FOOT OF THE MOUNTAINS OVER THOUSANDS OR MILLIONS OF YEARS. ALLUVIAL FANS ARE UNSAFE DURING A FLOOD BECAUSE IT'S EASY FOR WATER AND DEBRIS TO FLOW DOWN INTO THEM.

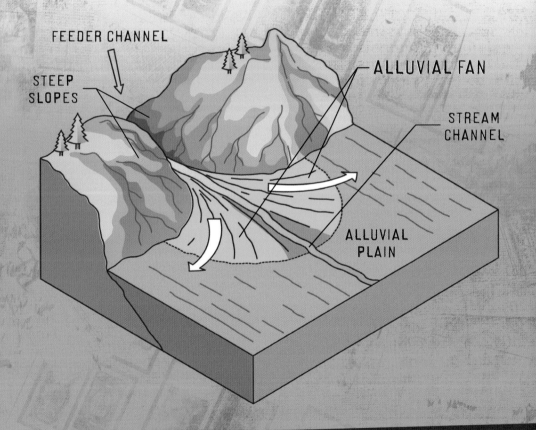

FEEDER CHANNEL

STEEP SLOPES

ALLUVIAL FAN

STREAM CHANNEL

ALLUVIAL PLAIN

⚠ THIS IS HOW ALLUVIAL FANS ARE SHAPED. WATER, DEBRIS, AND SEDIMENT COME DOWN THROUGH THE FEEDER CHANNEL TO SPREAD OVER THE ALLUVIAL PLAIN.

17

SOUTHEAST ASIA
IN 2011

The region of Southeast Asia often deals with severe floods. In 2011, the monsoon season, or time of very heavy rainfall, was especially serious. It caused flooding across many countries. Several intense storms also added to the flooding. Rivers overflowed, and the floodwaters damaged or destroyed homes, factories, and farmland. Around 1,300 people died throughout Southeast Asia.

Thailand and Cambodia were hit particularly hard. More than 500 people died in Thailand, and around 250 people died in Cambodia. More than half of Thailand flooded. In Thailand alone, the floods caused more than $40 billion of damage. It was the worst flooding Thailand had seen in decades.

IT WAS HARD TO LEAVE DURING THAILAND'S FLOOD IN 2011 BECAUSE MANY ROADS WERE CLOSED AND MANY PEOPLE WERE LEAVING AT THE SAME TIME.

BUSINESS IN THAILAND

THE FLOODS IN THAILAND AFFECTED BUSINESS AROUND THE WORLD. THAILAND IS A MAJOR PRODUCER OF RUBBER, RICE, AND COMPUTER HARD DRIVES. MORE THAN 25 PERCENT OF COMPUTER HARD DRIVES IN THE WORLD ARE MADE IN THAILAND. THE FLOODS SHUT DOWN MANY FACTORIES, WHICH CAUSED SUPPLY ISSUES FOR MONTHS.

INDIA'S TERRIBLE FLOOD

India is another Asian country that suffers from awful floods. In June 2013, India faced the deadliest flood it had seen in decades. Monsoon rain was falling in Northern India, and to make matters worse, a sudden, heavy storm called a cloudburst happened at the same time.

The high floodwaters and landslides severely damaged or destroyed buildings, roads, and entire villages. Around 70,000 people had to leave, and more than 6,000 people died. The floodwaters cut off many routes out of the area, trapping more than 50,000 people. In the days after the storms, thousands of rescue workers searched for ways to help those who had been stranded.

THIS PHOTO SHOWS ONE OF MANY TRIPS THE INDIAN AIR FORCE TOOK TO RESCUE STRANDED PEOPLE AFTER THE FLOODS IN JUNE 2013.

SEARCH AND RESCUE

THE INDIAN GOVERNMENT AND MILITARY WORKED FOR OVER A MONTH TO FIND AND RESCUE PEOPLE. THEY USED HELICOPTERS TO DROP OFF SUPPLIES AND FLY PEOPLE OUT OF FLOODED AREAS. BY THE MIDDLE OF JULY, MORE THAN 100,000 PEOPLE HAD BEEN RESCUED. IT WAS ONE OF THE INDIAN AIR FORCE'S LARGEST RESCUE MISSIONS IN HISTORY.

AMAZON RIVER
RISING

The Amazon River, one of the most famous rivers in the world, has been flooding more in the 21st century than ever before. Scientists began keeping track of river levels and floods in the Amazon **basin** in 1902. Even with records going back so far, seven of the ten worst floods in the area happened between 2009 and 2021 alone.

In May 2021, heavy rainfall flooded the basin and reached many towns, affecting around 450,000 people. The city of Manaus, Brazil, flooded badly. Many people either left the area or tried to adapt by raising their homes higher off the ground. The city even built wooden walkways above the water.

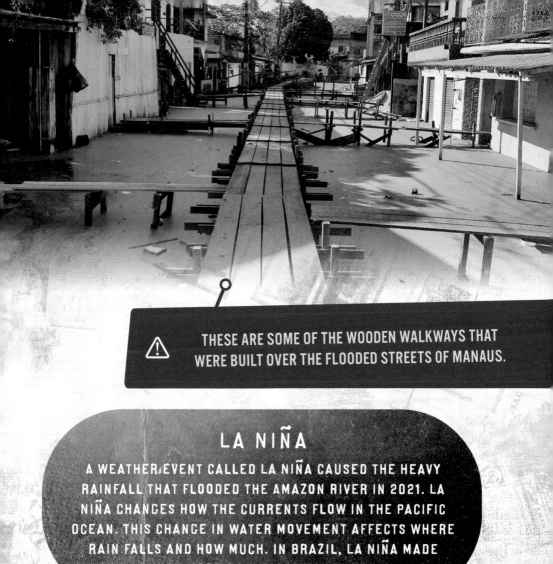

⚠ THESE ARE SOME OF THE WOODEN WALKWAYS THAT WERE BUILT OVER THE FLOODED STREETS OF MANAUS.

LA NIÑA

A WEATHER EVENT CALLED LA NIÑA CAUSED THE HEAVY RAINFALL THAT FLOODED THE AMAZON RIVER IN 2021. LA NIÑA CHANGES HOW THE CURRENTS FLOW IN THE PACIFIC OCEAN. THIS CHANGE IN WATER MOVEMENT AFFECTS WHERE RAIN FALLS AND HOW MUCH. IN BRAZIL, LA NIÑA MADE MUCH MORE RAIN FALL THAN USUAL.

MANAUS, BRAZIL, MAY 2021

FLOODS IN NIGERIA

In October 2022, intense floods gushed through the West African country of Nigeria. Heavy rainfall due to **climate change** was the main cause. The heavy rain also forced Nigeria and the nearby country of Cameroon to let excess water out of some dams so they wouldn't break, which added to the floods.

The disaster affected more than 2.8 million people. More than 1.3 million people were **displaced**, and over 600 people died. The floods destroyed more than 200,000 homes and damaged thousands of acres of farmland. It was the worst flooding Nigeria had seen in a decade. In 2012, floods had displaced more than 2 million people and killed 363 others.

THE 2012 FLOOD

NIGERIA HAS A RAINY SEASON THAT CAUSES SOME FLASH FLOODING EACH YEAR. HOWEVER, A FLOOD IN 2012 WAS THE WORST THE COUNTRY HAD SEEN IN ABOUT 50 YEARS. RIVERS SUCH AS THE NIGER, THE THIRD LONGEST RIVER IN AFRICA, OVERFLOWED SEVERELY. BETWEEN JULY AND NOVEMBER, AROUND 7.7 MILLION PEOPLE WERE AFFECTED BY THE FLOOD.

⚠ MANY COMMUNITIES FACED WIDESPREAD FLOODING IN 2022, INCLUDING THE ONE SEEN HERE IN NIGERIA'S ANAMBRA STATE.

FLOOD SAFETY

Flooding is a common problem. Controlling floods may be hard, but it is possible. Cities and towns use dams and dikes to keep water from reaching them. Some people build their houses high above the ground. Floods are a danger, but there are things you can do to stay safe.

If floods happen where you live, have supplies ready. Check the local news on TV, the radio, or online if there is danger of a flood. Leave home if you are told to and get to higher ground. Do not try to drive or walk through floodwaters. Make a plan with your family to meet at a certain spot if you get separated.

DISASTER PREPAREDNESS
CHECKLIST

☐ FIRST AID KIT
☐ FLASHLIGHT, RADIO AND SPARE BATTERIES
☐ BLANKETS, CLOTHES

 WHEN PACKING A DISASTER KIT, PUT YOUR SUPPLIES IN PLASTIC BAGS OR A WATERPROOF BACKPACK SO THEY DON'T GET WET.

BEING PREPARED

IT'S A GOOD IDEA TO LEARN HOW COMMON FLOODS ARE IN YOUR COMMUNITY. IF YOU LIVE IN A FLOOD-PRONE AREA, ASK YOUR PARENT OR GUARDIAN ABOUT KEEPING SUPPLIES SUCH AS BOTTLED WATER, PLASTIC SHEETING, SANDBAGS FOR BLOCKING FLOODWATERS, AND OTHER MATERIALS HANDY. BE MINDFUL OF ANY STREAMS, RIVERS, OR STORM DRAINS THAT MIGHT OVERFLOW IN THE EVENT OF A FLOOD.

CLIMATE
CHANGE

Scientists have found that climate change has been making floods worse. From 2000 to 2019, nearly half of all natural disasters were floods. In that time, around 1.6 billion people around the world were affected.

Climate change impacts many factors that make flooding worse, including heavy rainfall, storm frequency, and rising sea levels. Human activities, such as burning fossil fuels, is the main cause of climate change. Switching to other energy sources will help and prevent floods from getting worse. If governments, energy companies, and everyday people can slow climate change, make more structures able to withstand floods, and better prepare for floods, everyone will be safer.

⚠ THESE BARRIERS ARE PART OF THE MOSE SYSTEM IN VENICE, ITALY. THE BARRIERS DEFEND THE CITY FROM HIGH-TIDE WATERS.

FIGHTING FLOODS

ENGINEERS CAN DESIGN AND BUILD STRUCTURES THAT PUSH FLOODWATERS BACK OR ALLOW THEM TO PASS BY SAFELY. FOR EXAMPLE, IN VENICE, ITALY, THE GOVERNMENT WORKED ON THE MOSE SYSTEM OF BARRIERS AGAINST HIGH-TIDE WATERS FOR NEARLY 40 YEARS. IN 2020, VENICE STARTED TO USE THE MOSE SYSTEM AND FOUND IT HELPED PREVENT FLOODS IN THE CITY.

GLOSSARY

basin: A dip in Earth's surface, somewhat shaped like a bowl. Also, an area that drains water from surrounding land.

climate change: Long-term change in Earth's climate, caused mainly by human activities such as burning oil and natural gas.

damage: Harm. Also, to cause harm.

debris: The remains of something that has been broken.

dike: A bank of dirt or sandbags built to control water.

disasters: Events that cause much suffering or loss.

displaced: Moved out of the usual position.

famine: Severe shortage of food.

ice jams: Blockages in which large pieces of ice clump together and block a river's flow.

levees: Raised riverbanks used to stop a river from overflowing.

recede: Go down or become less.

sediment: Matter, such as stones and sand, that is carried onto land or into the water by wind, water, or land movement.

storm surge: The rise of water above the usual tide, caused by a storm.

FOR MORE INFORMATION

BOOKS

Burg, Ann E. *Flooded: Requiem for Johnstown.* New York, NY: Scholastic, 2022.

Spilsbury, Louise. *The Science Behind Super Floods.* Shrewsbury, UK: Cheriton Children's Books, 2022.

Williams, Olivia. *Understanding Floods.* Ann Arbor, MI: Cherry Lake Publishing, 2022.

WEBSITES

National Severe Storms Library
nssl.noaa.gov/education/students
Learn more about severe weather, floods, and disasters with activities, worksheets, and more.

NOAA SciJinks: Water and Ice
scijinks.gov/menu/water-and-ice
Learn more about the different causes of floods and how they affect our world.

Ready Kids
ready.gov/kids/disaster-facts/floods
Learn more about what to do before, during, and after a flood.

INDEX